AMERICAN HEAVY CRUISER NEW ORLEAN CLASS
USS "VINCENNES" CA-44 1942

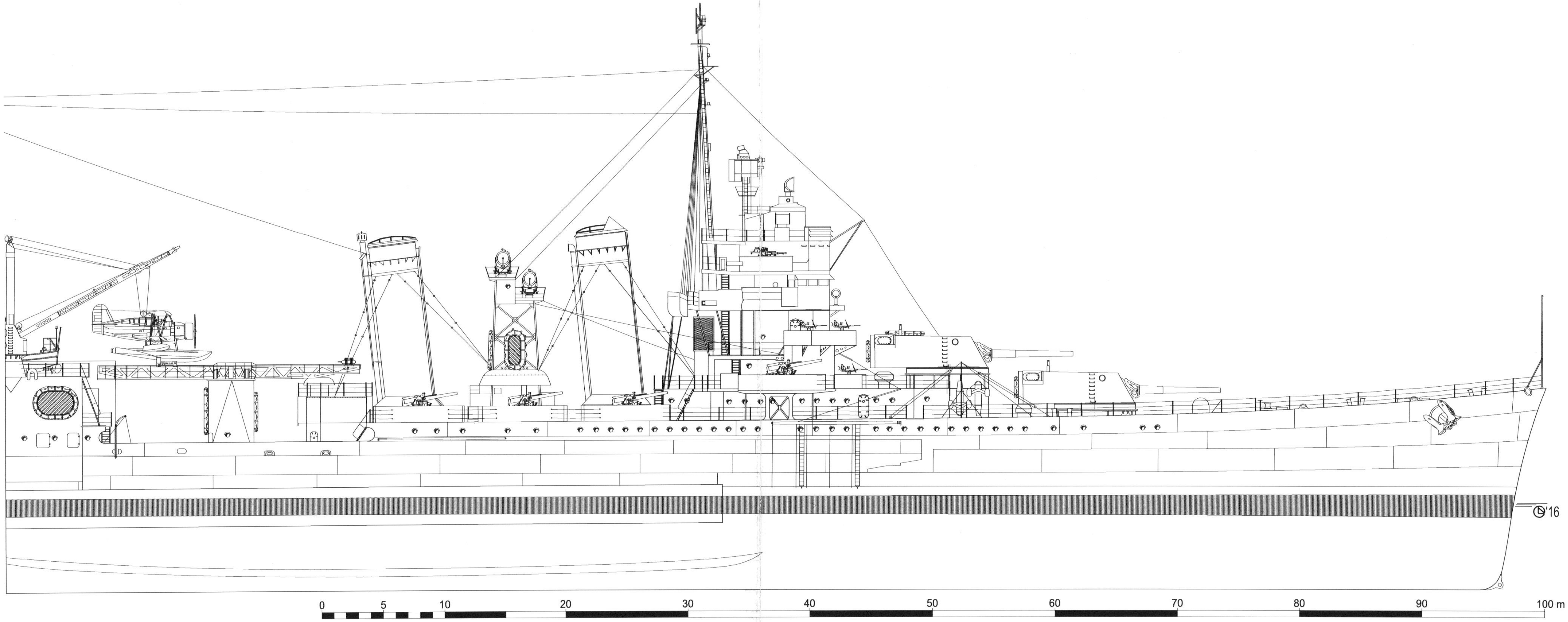

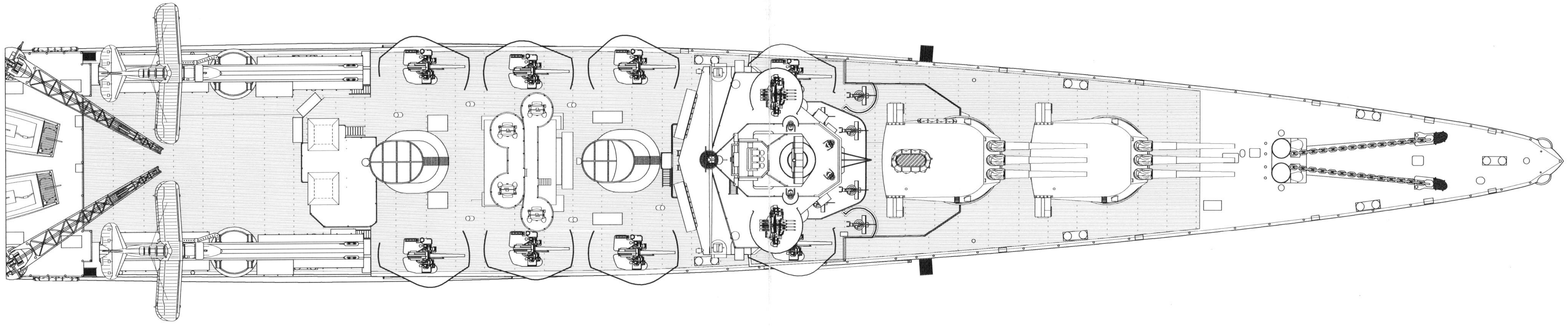

AMERICAN HEAVY CRUISER NEW ORLEAN CLASS
USS "VINCENNES" CA-44 1942

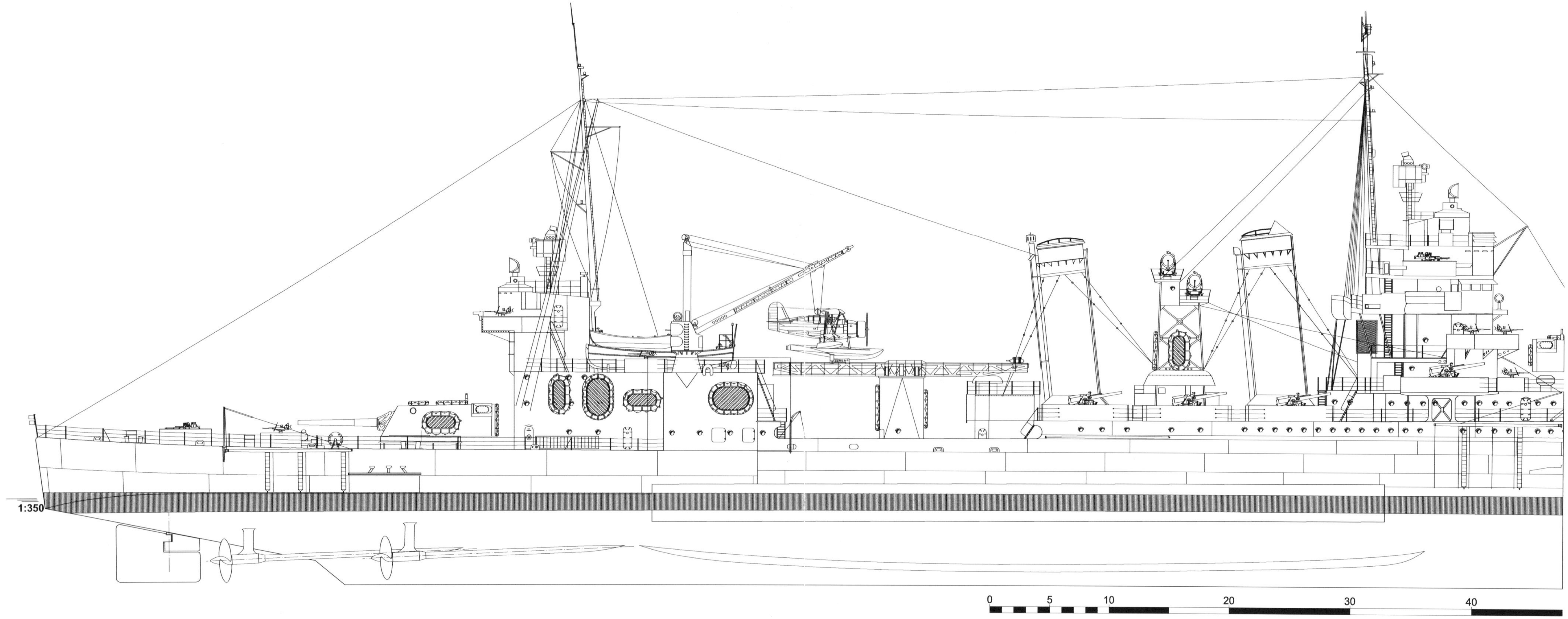

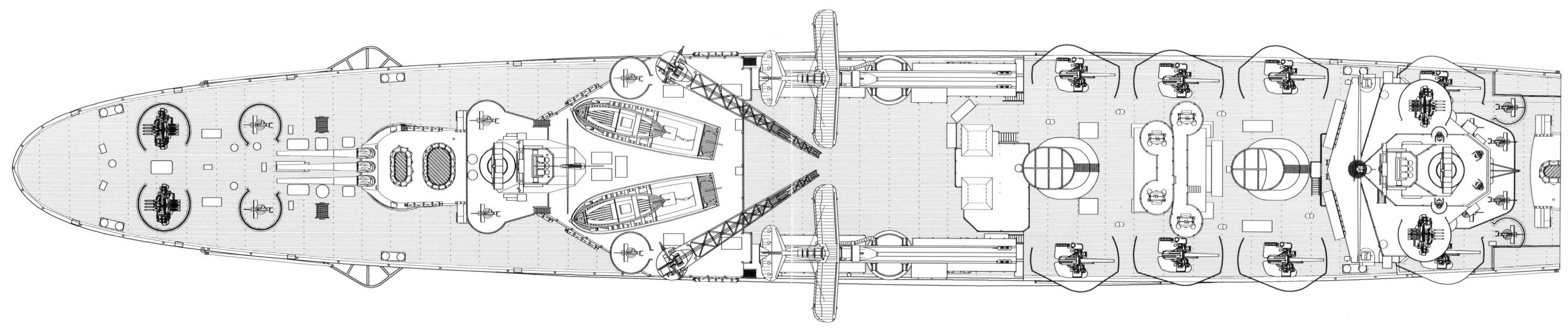

1/350 Scale Plans

**AMERICAN HEAVY CRUISER NEW ORLEAN CLASS
USS "VINCENNES" CA-44 1942
MAIN DECK AND UPPER DECK PLAN**

UPPER DECK PLAN

MAIN & WELL DECK PLAN

SHIP'S BOW VIEW

PROPPELER GUARD

BOLLARD (1:175 Scale)

PROPPELER

STOWAGE, AVIATION WORKSHOP & STOREROOM, CREW'S WASHROOMS & W.C.

TOP VIEW

TOP VIEW

BOW VIEW

1,1' GUN SHIELD ON MAIN DECK

TOP VIEW

STERN VIEW

BOW VIEW PORTSIDE VIEW STERN VIEW STARBOARD VIEW PORTSIDE VIEW STERN VIEW STARBOARD VIEW

SHIP' STERN VIEW

STARBOARD VIEW

© Grzegorz Nowak 2016

AMERICAN HEAVY CRUISER NEW ORLEAN CLASS
USS "VINCENNES" CA-44 1942
HULL LINES AND BODY PLAN

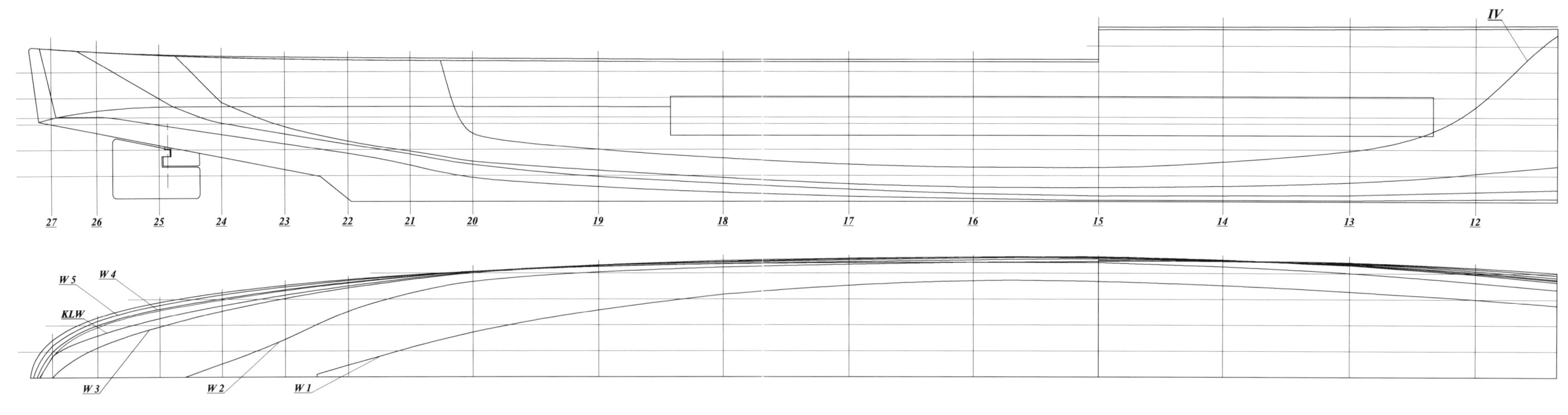
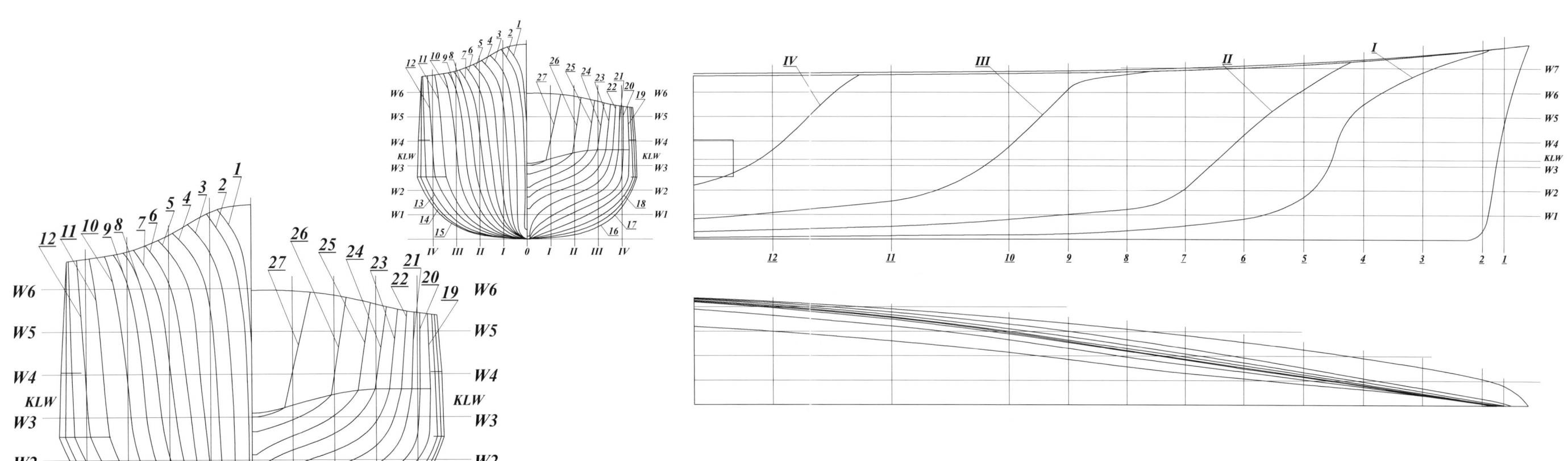

© Grzegorz Nowak 2016

1/350 Scale Plans

AMERICAN HEAVY CRUISER NEW ORLEAN CLASS
USS "VINCENNES" CA-44 1942
SUPERSTRUCTURE & MIDSHIP LEVELS & FUNNELS

CONSTRUCTION OF SUPERSTRUCTURE

TOP VIEW

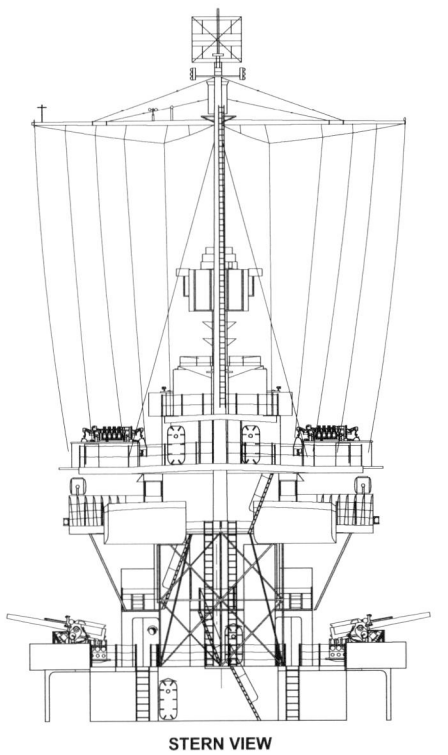
STERN VIEW

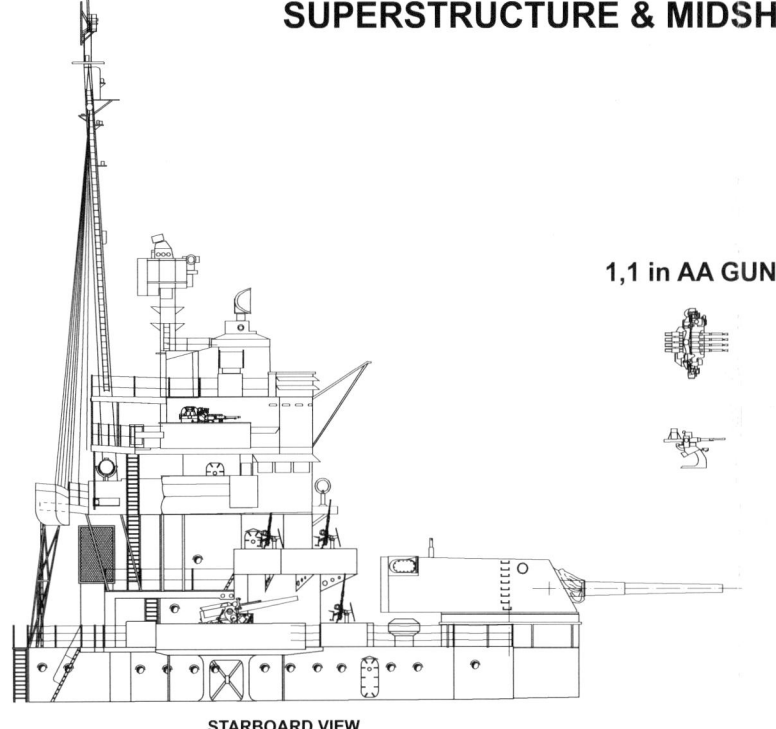
STARBOARD VIEW

1,1 in AA GUN

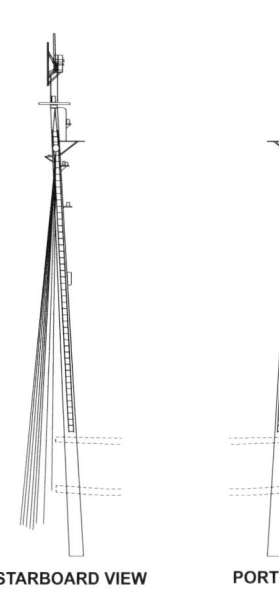

MAIN MAST & S.C. AIR SEARCH RADAR ANTENNA

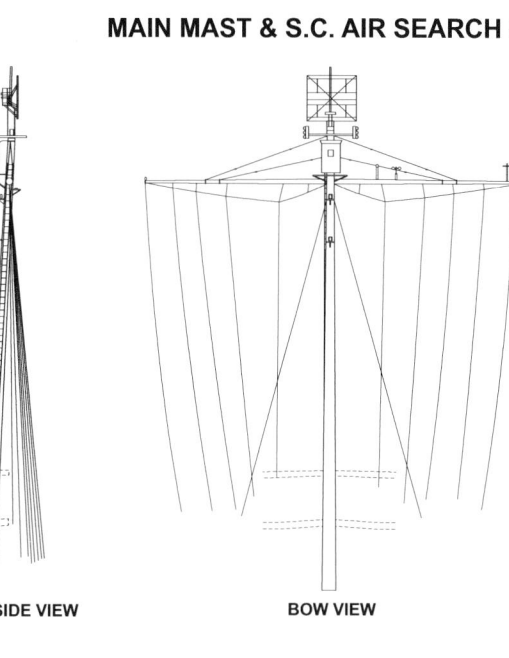
STARBOARD VIEW — PORTSIDE VIEW

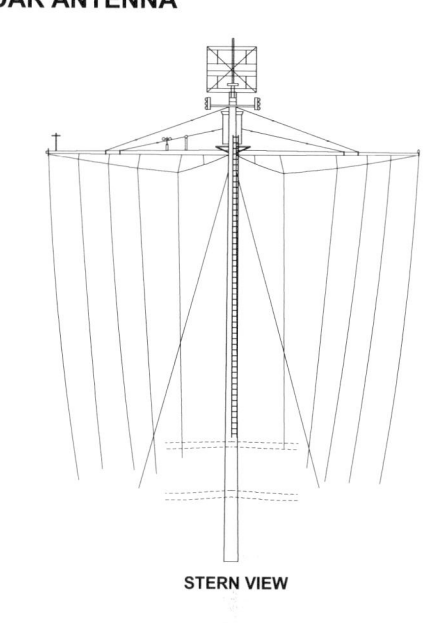
BOW VIEW — STERN VIEW

36 in SEARCHLIGHT

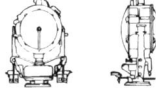

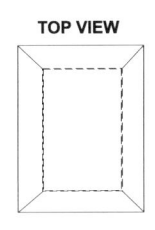
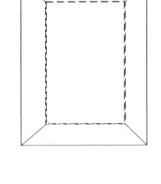
TOP VIEW

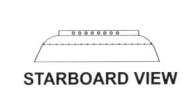
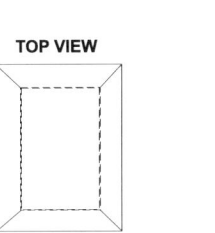
STERN VIEW — STARBOARD VIEW — BOW VIEW — PORTSIDE VIEW

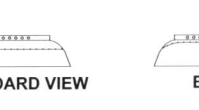

Podstawa

SEARCHLIGT PLATFORMS

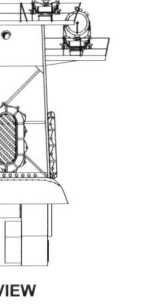 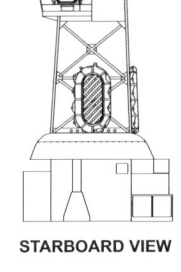 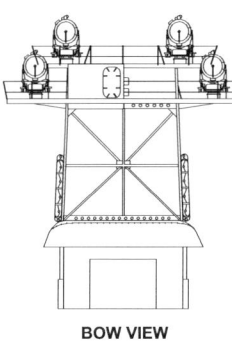 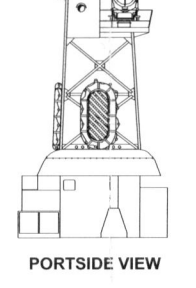
STERN VIEW — STARBOARD VIEW — BOW VIEW — PORTSIDE VIEW

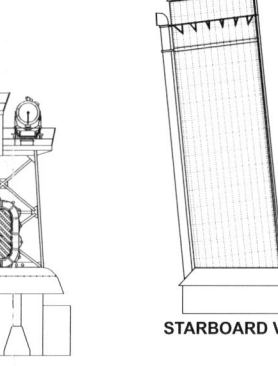
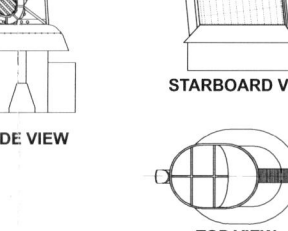
Widok z góry na platformę reflektorów

Podstawa nadbudówki reflektorów skala 1:250

MAIN FUNNEL

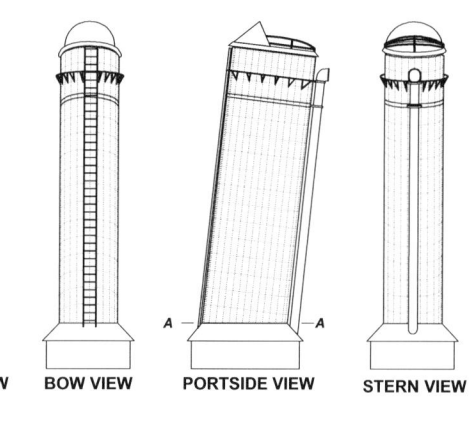
STARBOARD VIEW — BOW VIEW — PORTSIDE VIEW — STERN VIEW

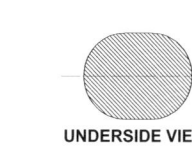 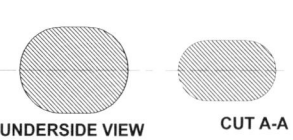
TOP VIEW — UNDERSIDE VIEW — CUT A-A

40 Ft. MOTOR LAUNCH

CATAPULT TOWERS (STARBOARD)

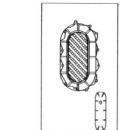 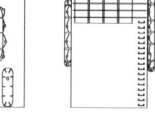 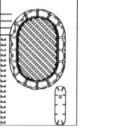 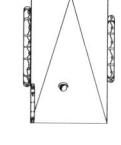
BOW VIEW — PORTSIDE VIEW — STERN VIEW — STARBOARD VIEW

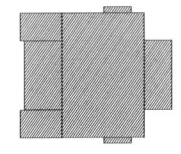
Widok od rufy — Widok z prawej — Widok od dziobu — Widok z lewej

26' MOTOR WHALEBOAT

AFT. FUNNEL

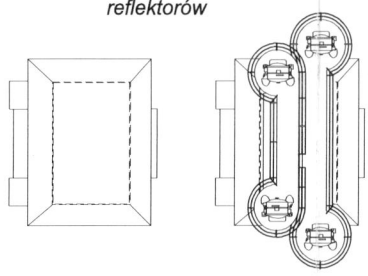
STARBOARD VIEW — BOW VIEW — PORTSIDE VIEW — STERN VIEW

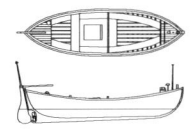
TOP VIEW — UNDERSIDE VIEW — CUT A-A

CATAPULT TOWERS (PORT SIDE)

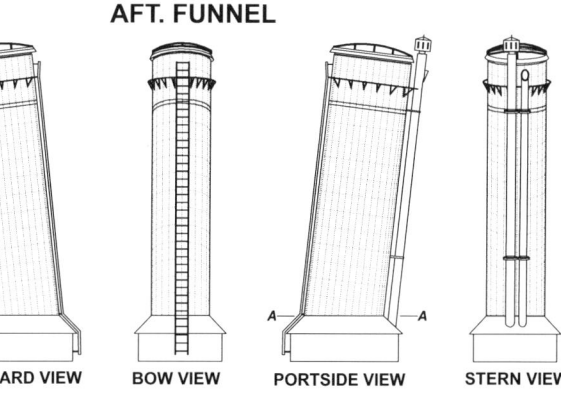

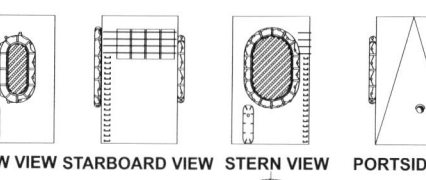
BOW VIEW — STARBOARD VIEW — STERN VIEW — PORTSIDE VIEW

 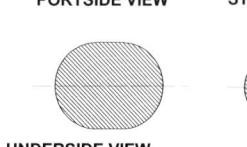 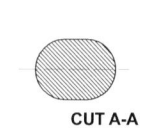

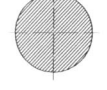

© Grzegorz Nowak 2016

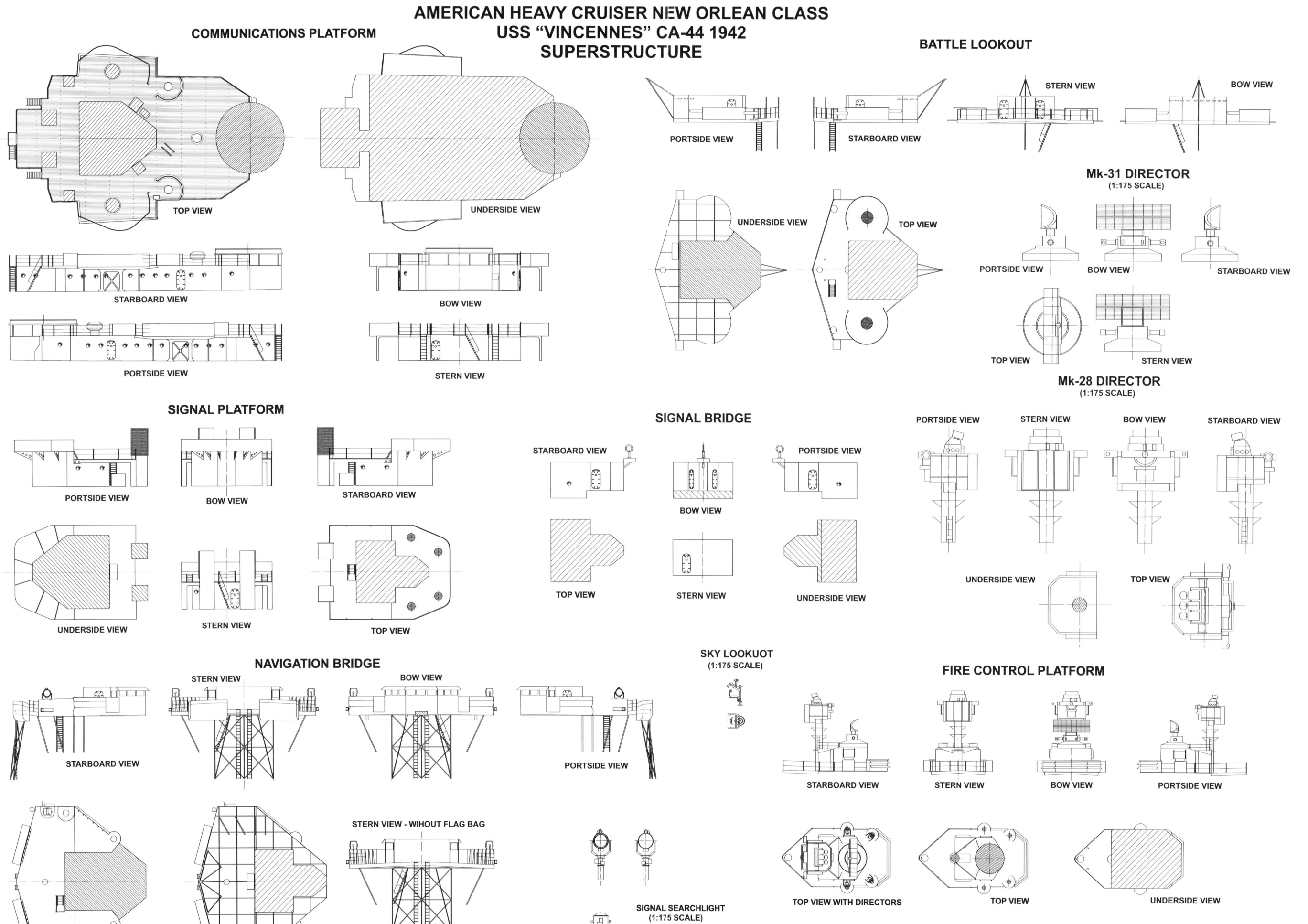

1/200 Scale Plans

AMERICAN HEAVY CRUISER NEW ORLEAN CLASS
USS "VINCENNES" CA-44 1942

AMERICAN HEAVY CRUISER NEW ORLEAN CLASS
USS "VINCENNES" CA-44 1942
HANGAR, AICRAFT CATAPULT, MOTOR LAUNCH STOWAGE, CHANDLING CRANE, ARMAMENT etc.

1/350 Scale Plans

CONSTRUCTION OF HANGAR

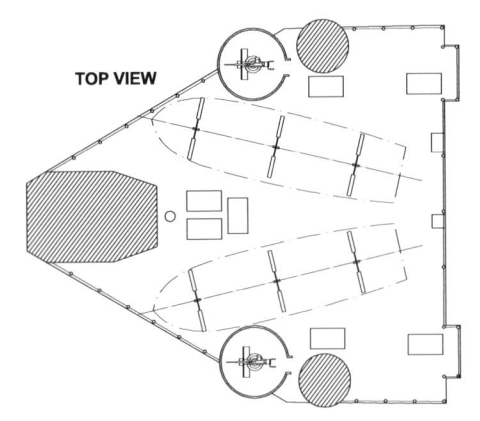

TOP VIEW

HANDLING CRANES

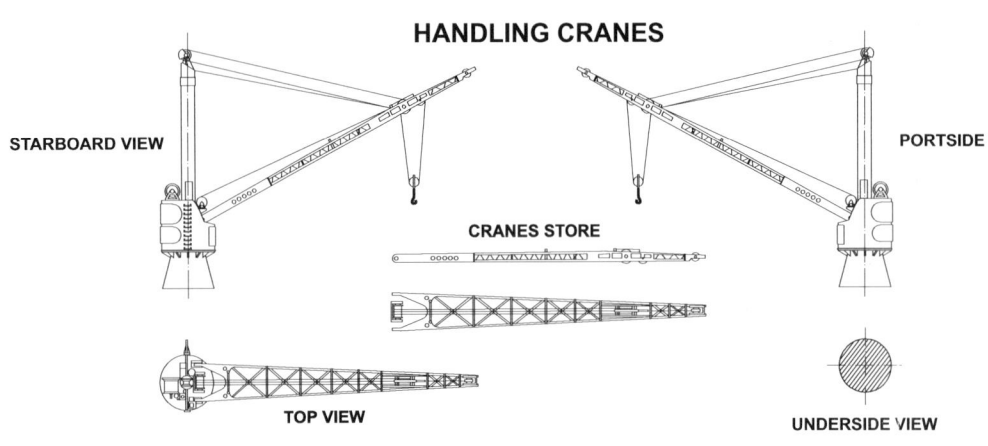

STARBOARD VIEW — PORTSIDE VIEW
CRANES STORE
TOP VIEW — UNDERSIDE VIEW

SHIP'S LIFE RAFTS

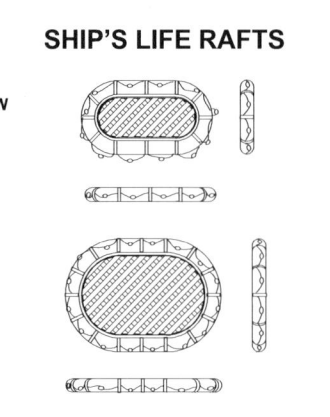

TRIPLE TURRET FOR 8in/55 GUN

5in/25 GUN

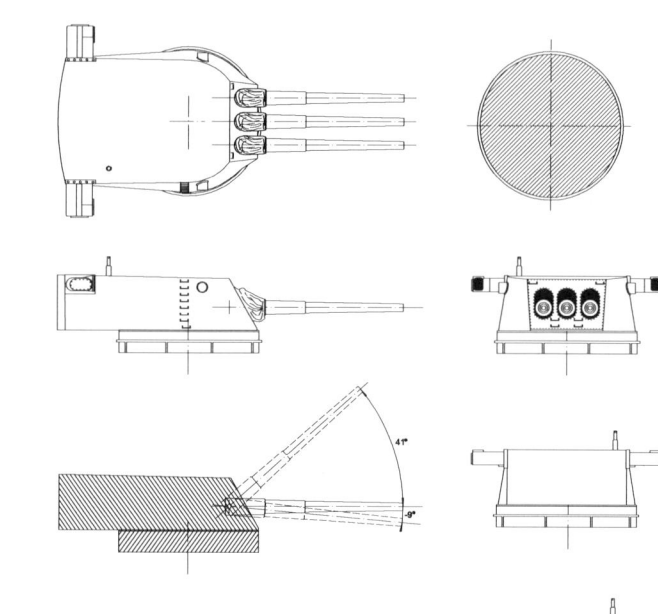

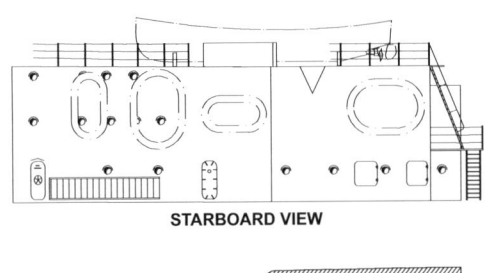

STARBOARD VIEW

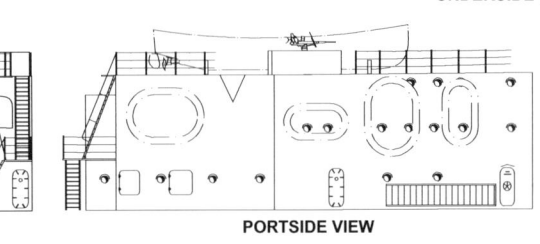

BOW VIEW — PORTSIDE VIEW — STERN VIEW

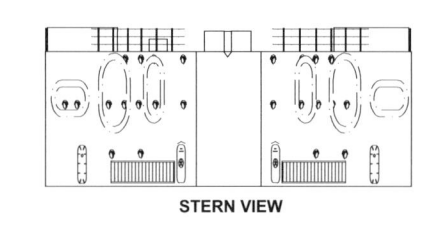

20 mm OERLIKON SINGLE MOUNT (1:175 Scale)

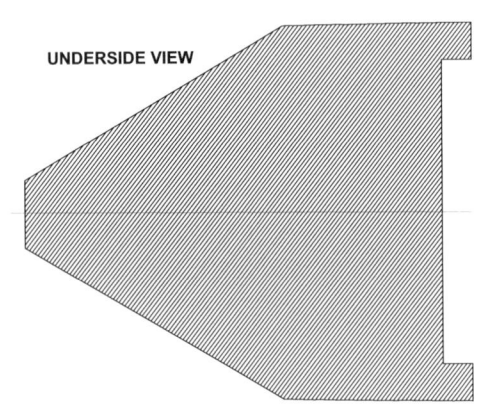

UNDERSIDE VIEW

AFT. FIRE CONTROL PLATFORM TOP

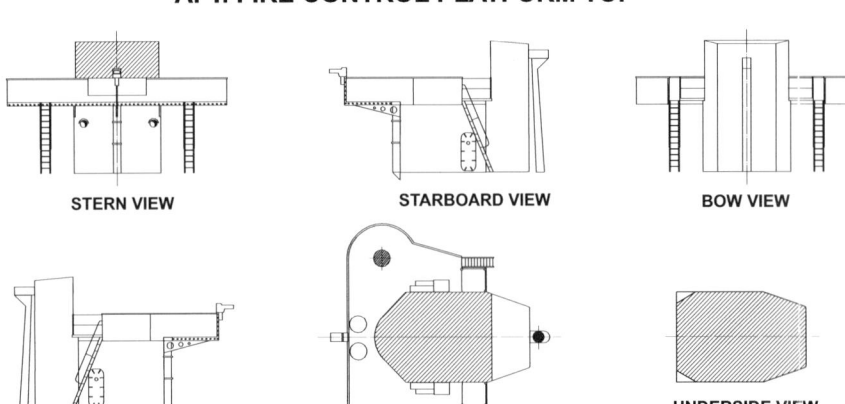

STERN VIEW — STARBOARD VIEW — BOW VIEW
PORTSIDE VIEW — TOP VIEW — UNDERSIDE VIEW

TOP VIEW

AFT. MAST

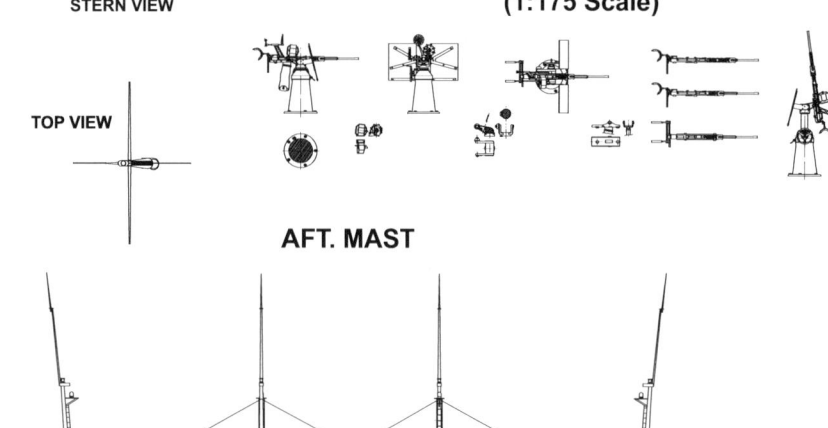

STARBOARD VIEW — BOW VIEW — STERN VIEW — PORTSIDE VIEW

CURTIS SOC "SEAGULL" FLOATPLANE

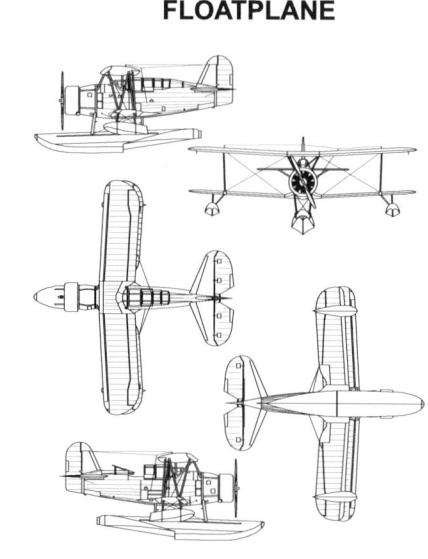

CATAPULT

TOP VIEW WITHOUT WALKWAYS
STARBOARD VIEW WITHOUT WALKWAYS
STARBOARD VIEW WITH WALKWAYS
TOP VIEW WITH WALKWAYS

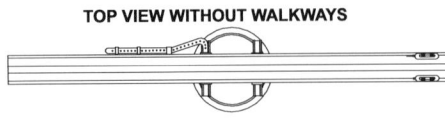

AFT. FIRE CONTROL PLATFORM TOP

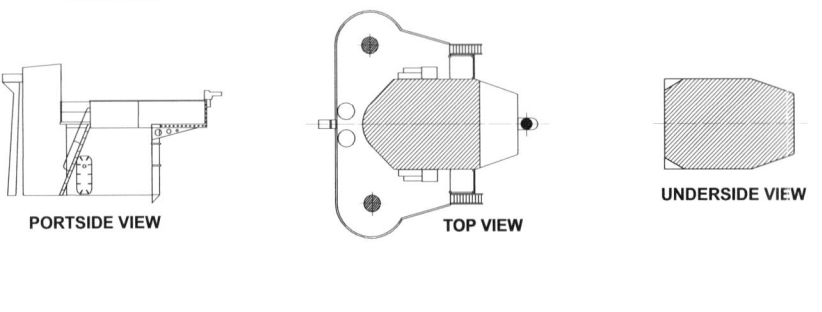

PORTSIDE VIEW WITH DIRECTORS — STERN VIEW — PORTSIDE VIEW — BOW VIEW
UNDERSIDE VIEW — TOP VIEW — STARBOARD VIEW

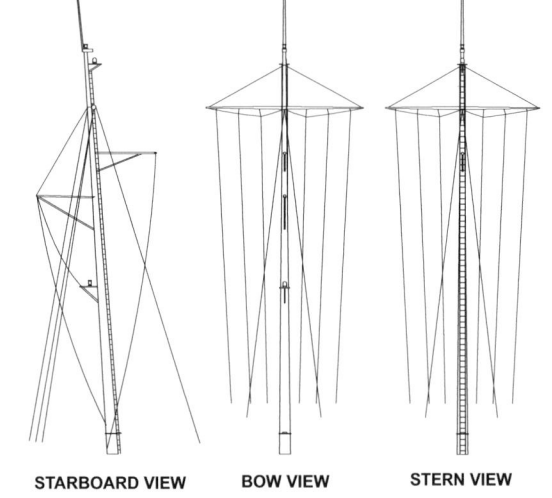

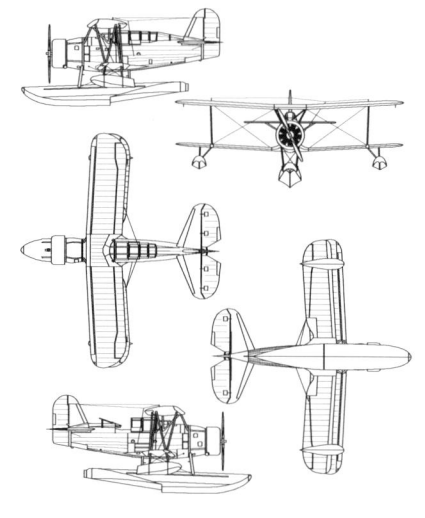

STERN SWINGING BOOM

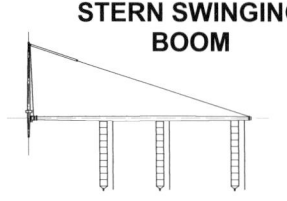

AMIDSHIP SWINGING BOOM

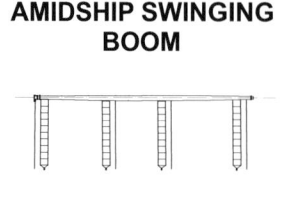

FORWARD SWINGING BOOM

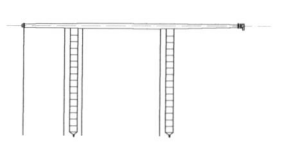

© Grzegorz Nowak 2016

AMERICAN HEAVY CRUISER NEW ORLEAN CLASS
USS "VINCENNES" CA-44 1942

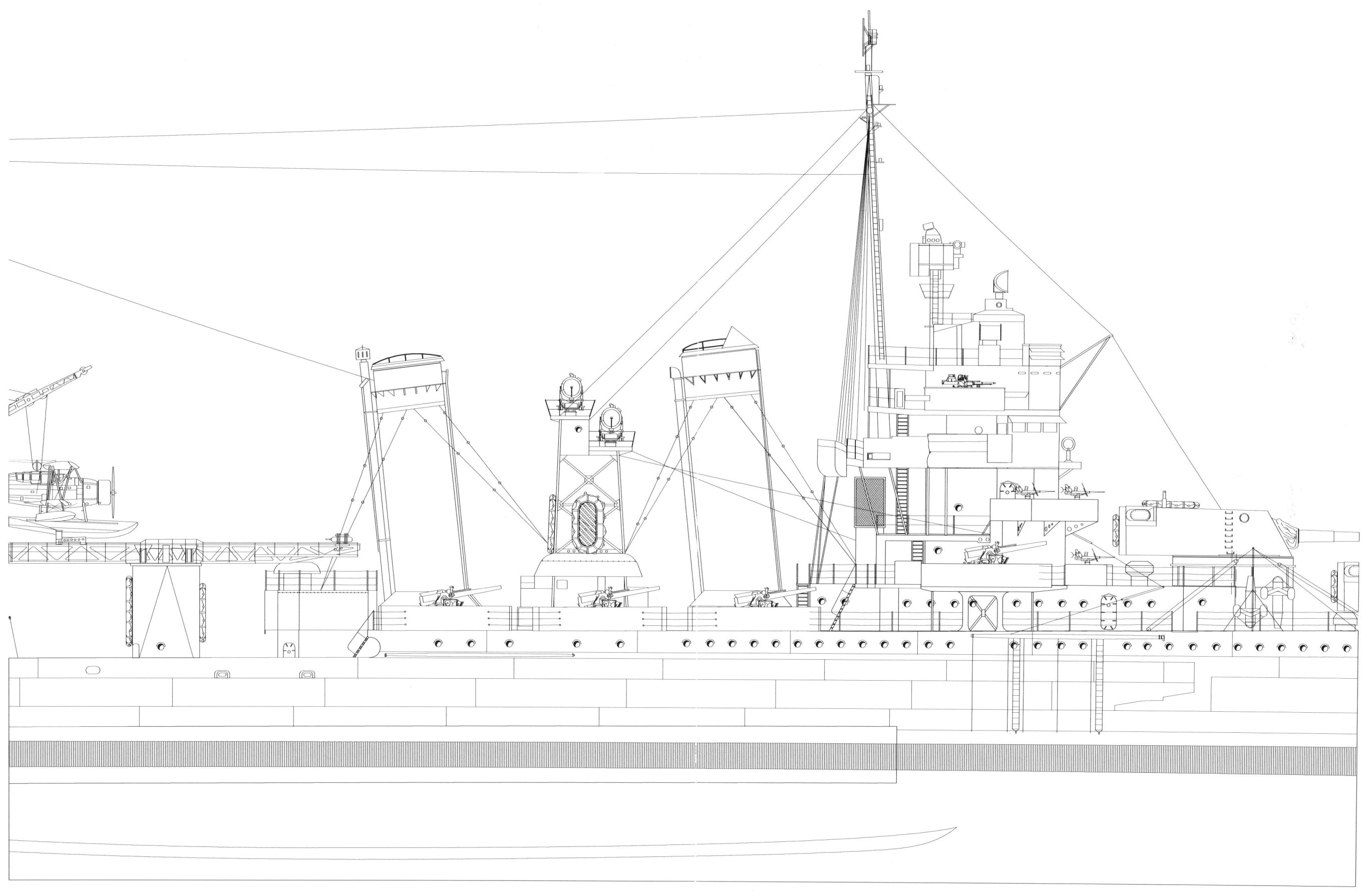

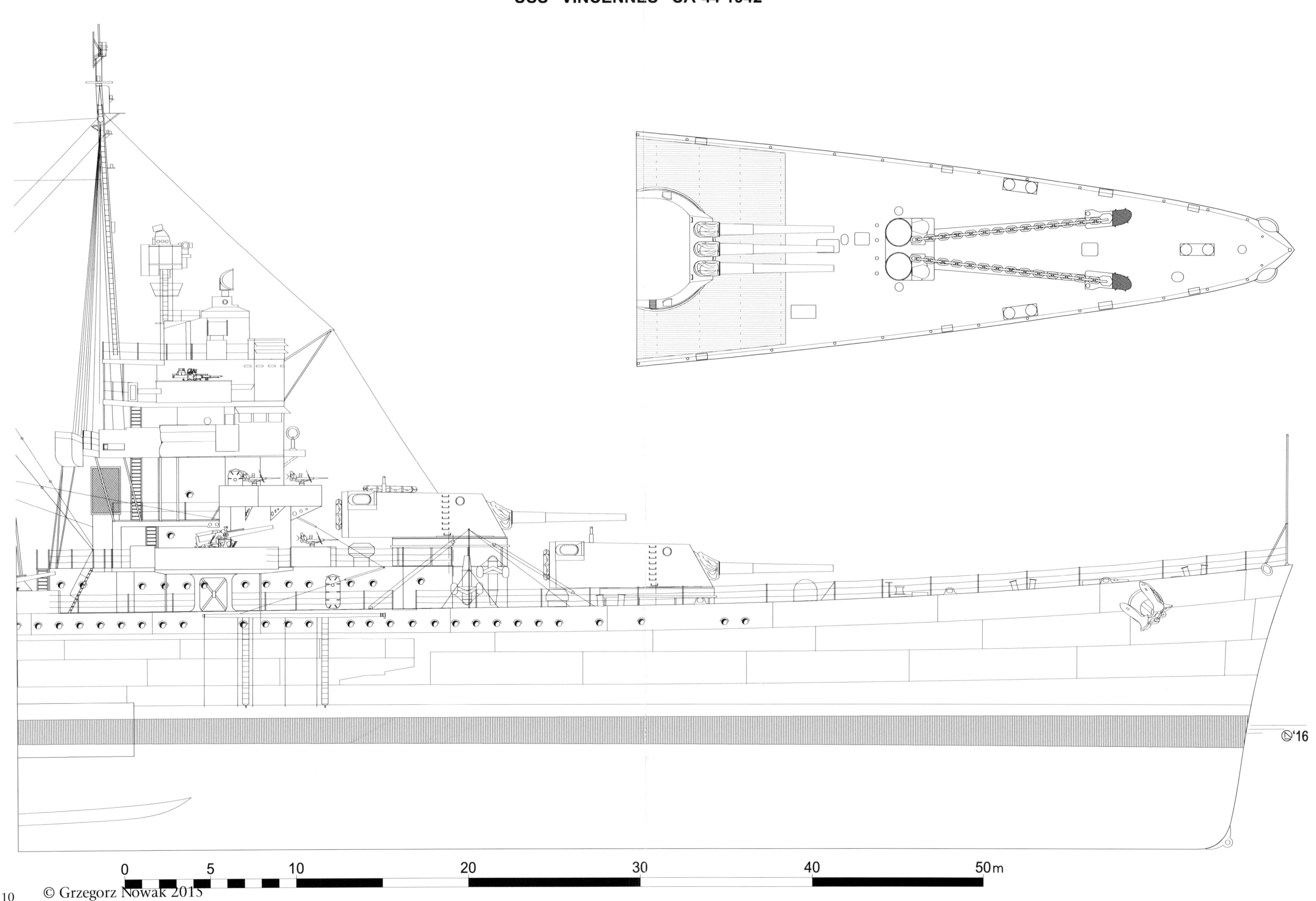

AMERICAN HEAVY CRUISER NEW ORLEAN CLASS
USS "VINCENNES" CA-44 1942

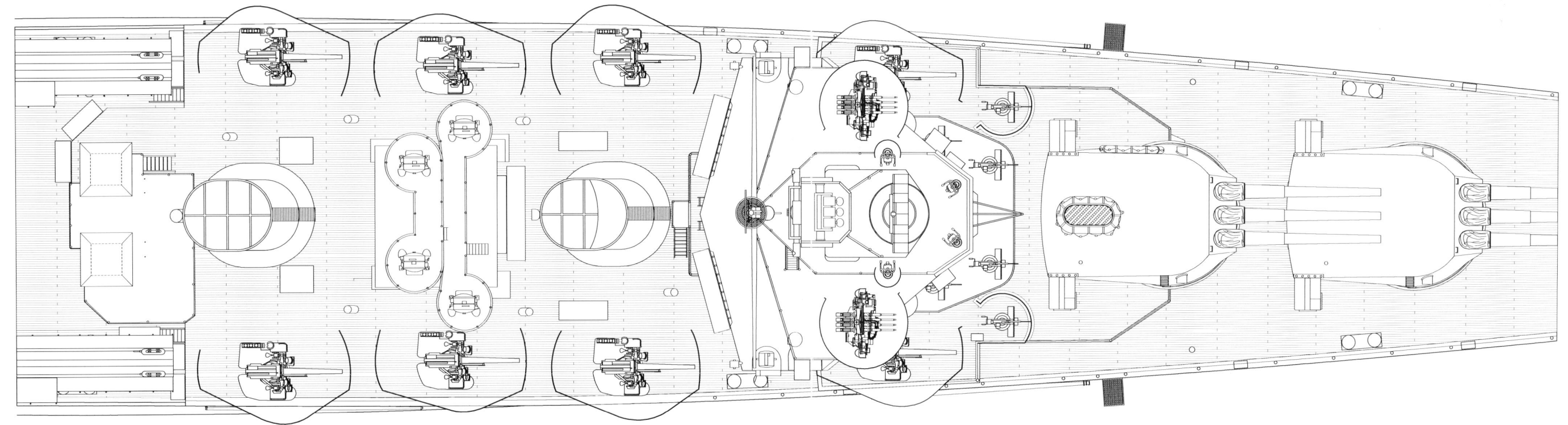

AMERICAN HEAVY CRUISER NEW ORLEAN CLASS
USS "VINCENNES" CA-44 1942

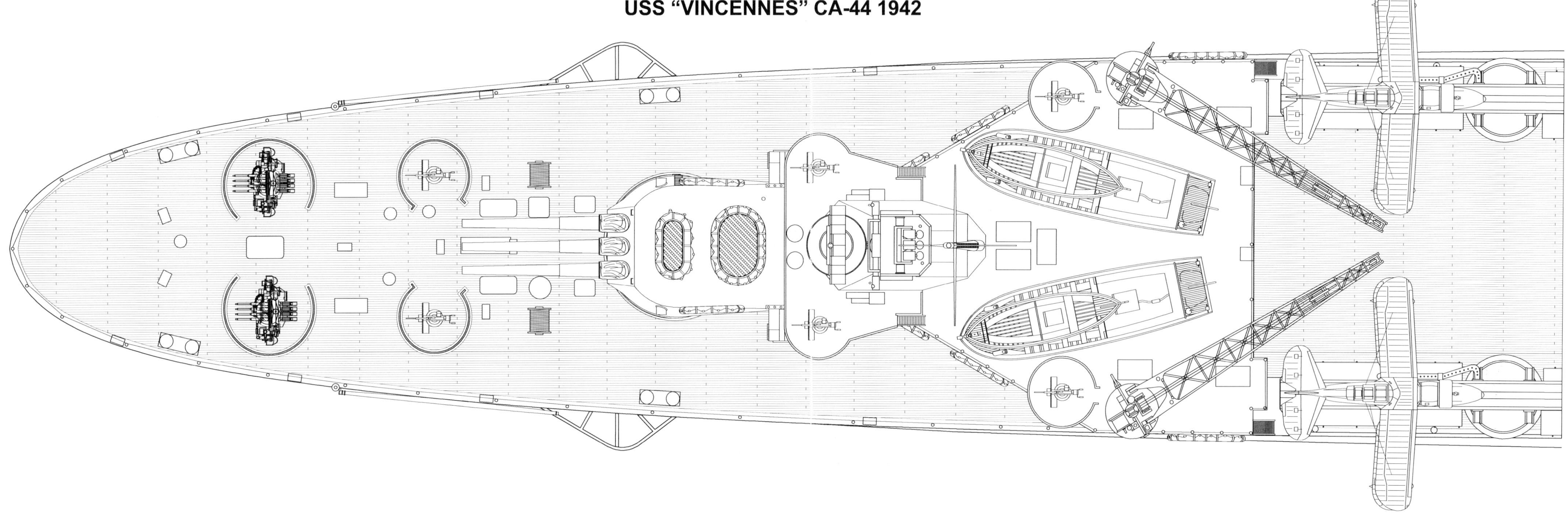

1/700 Scale Plans

USS VINCENNES (CA-44) SPECIFICATIONS (as completed)

Displacement	9 375 tons (std)	11 527 tons (full load)
Lenght	179,22 m. (overall)	176,17 m (WL)
Beam	18,8 m.	
Draft	5,9 m	
Machinery	4 x Parsons type Turbine	107 000 SHP
Boilers	8 x Babcok & Wilcox type boiler	
Speed	32,75 kts.	
Range	7 600 nm at 15 kts	3 500 nm at 25 kts
Fuel	2 270 tons	
Crew	807	

ARNAMENT (1942)

Main battery	9 x 203 mm	8 in./55 cal (2 x III)
Heavy AA guns	8 x 127 mm	5 in./25 cal (8 x I)
Light AA guns	16 x 28 mm	1,1in. (4 x IV)
	12 x 20 mm	20 mm Oerlikon (12 x I)
Catapults	2	
Aircraft	4 (SOC „Seagull")	

AMERICAN HEAVY CRUISER NEW ORLEAN CLASS
USS "VINCENNES" CA-44 1942
1:700 scale

NEW ORLEANS CLASS HEAVY CRUISERS

Name		Keel Laid	Launched	Commissioned	Fate
USS "NEW ORLEANS"	CA-32	14.03.1931	12.04.1933	15.02.1934	Scrapped
USS "ASTORIA"	CA-34	01.09.1930	16.12.1933	28.04.1934	Sunk 09.08.1942
USS "MINNEAPOLIS"	CA-36	27.01.1931	06.09.1933	19.05.1934	Scrapped
USS "TUSCALLOSA"	CA-37	03.09.1931	15.11.1933	17.08.1934	Scrapped
USS "SAN FRANCISCO"	CA-38	09.09.1931	09.03.1933	10.02.1934	Scrapped
USS "QUINCY"	CA-39	15.11.1933	19.06.1935	09.06.1936	Sunk 09.08.1942
USS "VINCENNES"	CA-44	02.01.1934	21.05.1936	24.02.1937	Sunk 09.08.1942

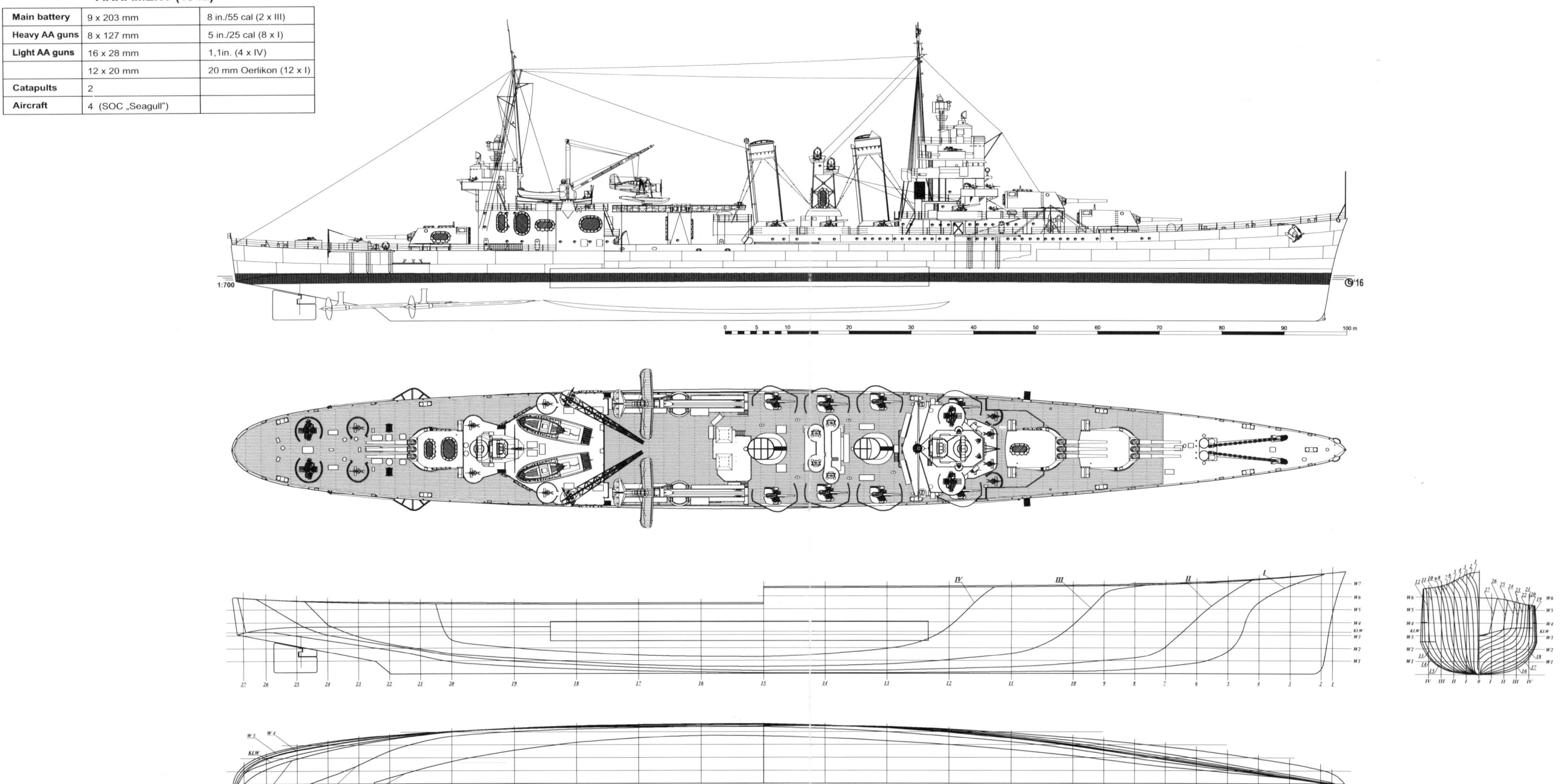

© Grzegorz Nowak 2015